The Inner Eye

15 January—19 February 1978

Museum of Modern Art Oxford 1978

Acknowledgements

In organising this exhibition Museum staff have been dependent upon the guidance, enthusiasm and energy of many art therapists and doctors who all have freely given their advice and time.

The gathering of such a large submission of work from hospitals and clinics from over the whole of the country obviously presents considerable practical problems, however, these have been greatly eased by the thoughtfulness and care of all those that have helped.

Michael Edwards, Diana Halliday, John Henzell and Peter Byrne offered invaluable guidance and advice in the early stages. Edward Adamson has kindly allowed us to borrow work from his own collection and Dr Raymond Levy has arranged for the loan of work from the Guttmann Maclay collection from the Institute of Psychiatry, University of London. John Evans, head of the art therapy department at Hertfordshire College of Art and Design, has also lent work from his collection and has put us in contact with other art therapists in hospitals. Patricia Allderidge, archivist at the Royal Bethlem Hospital, has given useful advice.

The therapists from hospitals which have submitted work could not have been more helpful and many have supplied full notes to accompany the work. The names of all the art therapists and hospitals appear in the catalogue section of this publication. I should like to thank them all for their trouble and concern.

John Henzell and Professor Richard Wollheim have kindly agreed to give lectures on related subjects and the open seminar has been organised with the help of the organisers of art therapy courses at Goldsmith's College, London, Hertfordshire College of Art and Design, St. Albans, and Birmingham Polytechnic.

Jenny Hackett, Robin Holton and Pat Nowell-Hall have also agreed to lead art therapy workshops during the exhibition.

Christine Newton, the Museum's Education Officer has been responsible for the organisation of the exhibition.

Lastly we should like to thank all of the artists who have allowed us to show their work.

Contents

Illustration 1

Nijinsky

Introduction

It is the policy of the Museum not only to show recent developments in the visual arts, placing these within a twentieth century art historical context, but also to examine different modes of non-verbal communication—different aspects of visual language.

Much of our previous work in this field has been linked with exhibitions of art made in schools and colleges grouped around the general heading of art education. This exhibition is more specifically directed, though the concept of education is still a central concern. This selection of work, made in psychiatric hospitals and clinics throughout the country shows how confused or suppressed inner feelings can be clarified or sublimated through expression as 'art'. Many of these images were made spontaneously, others resulted from contact with an art therapist. The meaning of this work is not always immediately clear (the same is true of dreams—another aspect of the creativity of the subconscious) however the sympathetic help and guidance of the art therapist over a period of time can encourage the patient (by his own effort) to begin to recognise and come to terms with his problems. In this sense art therapy or even just art creativity provides the opportunity for self-realisation, self-education—and in some cases self-healing.

In the art therapeutic relationship awareness does not flow only from the therapist to the patient. It is essential that the reverse also takes place so that the wider meanings of symbols, conventions and forms in the work can be clarified in discussion with the patient. Everything we do has a meaning which relates to our whole personality—our walk, our choice of clothes and colours, the way we write, say things or draw a line. The meaning of what we do can only be properly understood within the context of our personality and the external circumstances in which we live. The work in this exhibition is essentially an art of communication—a transmission, often unconscious, of deeply held beliefs, fears, fantasies and obsessions. For some patients, made, drawn, or painted objects are the only means of communication.

Ultimately we all have our own languages—visual, verbal, physical—it takes time and care from someone else to get to know what we really mean. We go through our lives leaving clues and signs for others to interpret.

In presenting this exhibition, we have had to strike a balance between letting work speak for itself (in a large number of cases there can be little ambiguity of meaning) and supplying contextual information to clarify meanings. In a way we have to make a similar kind of decision with all the exhibitions shown at the Museum especially when we consider that the 'language' of an artist's work may not be easily understood by a large proportion of our visitors.

Much of the work, especially the case histories, is concerned with radical development and change. This is usually a function of successful treatment. It is dynamic, disquieting and little of it is concerned with conventional aesthetic notions of beauty and harmony which many people regard as a prerequisite of 'good art'.

The technical expertise of patients whose work is shown varies widely; a number of patients have had previous art training and usually this is evident from the work. A number of 'Fine Art' references do appear in patients' work—often in that of patients who have had no formal artistic training. This probably derives from the small 'libraries' of art books that art therapists have collected in their departments. Work from severely physically handicapped patients has not been included as it was felt that their physical disabilities restricted their possibilities of communication; this would have confused the issues central to this exhibition.

This exhibition was selected from a large submission of work sent in by art therapists. The nature and content of the work defies classification according to conventional art world criteria. The criteria of selection have been inevitably those of compromise. However, a rough marriage has been made between the clinically and visually interesting and, fortunately, these interests did not often appear to clash. The works are displayed in the Museum with a view to their visual cohesiveness; certain kinds of disorder do seem to lead to particular forms of expression. Works are exhibited in series if this elucidates their meaning as in the example of case histories or in the work of obsessive patients. A number of examples of group work are also displayed with some gloss on the relationships which developed during the making of the work. Many therapists also like to use some visual *leitmotif* upon which patients can extemporise—to serve as a basis for discussion in psychotherapy. A series of such theme paintings made by both therapists and patients is shown. Much work in this exhibition, however, was not consciously made as art although it may appear as such to us or even in retrospect may be regarded as such by the patient. (Some psychologists would argue the roots of all creativity are essentially pathological—art results from an attempt to heal the damaged Self.) Certainly the efforts of Jean Dubuffet over the past thirty years and his assembly of a large collection of psychotic art (*art brut*) have done much to change the climate of public opinion towards such intense private work. (The question of the relationship of such work to other concepts of art is discussed below in greater detail by Peter Byrne and John Henzell.)

Art therapy in this country has really only developed since the war and as yet there is no public collection of psychopathological art to rival Dubuffet's collection, now in Switzerland, or the collection assembled by Hans Prinzhorn which is kept in Heidelberg.
To date, two significant collections of psychopathological art, of which there are examples in this exhibition, have been made in this country: the Guttmann Maclay collection administered by the Institute of Psychiatry, University of London, and the collection of some 70,000 works assembled by Edward Adamson whilst working as art therapist at the Netherne Hospital in Coulsdon, Surrey. It is hoped that in the future a national collection of psychopathological art may be formed perhaps using the excellent resources of these collections as a basis.
The intensity of the images in this exhibition is overpowering—their implications are shattering. A similar intensity and possibility for creativity exists in all of us. This exhibition is a tribute to those who have let us see their work.

David Elliott
Director

Illustration 2

Art and Madness

Peter Byrne

'The Inner Eye' contains pictures made by people in hospitals and clinics or under some form of treatment for what we call mental illness. These pictures are obviously interesting in many respects, but are they works of art?

The art gallery visitor has become used to two types of exhibition. The first presents the work of an acknowledged master, a school, or a period; and generally speaking the artistic status of what is shown is not in question. The second presents works whose claim to artistic validity has still to be proven (most *avant-garde* exhibitions belong to this type). 'The Inner Eye' fits into neither of these categories. This collection of images does not show the development of a style in art, nor is it the work of an established school; it does not belong to a particular historical period, nor is it *avant-garde*. And what of the people who have produced the work? Some have had a training in art, others have not touched a pencil or brush between leaving primary school and finding themselves in hospital.

The question seems to bear on common assumptions about what art is, and what its function in society may be. Further it links itself with a wider-ranging critique of the art world and its values. Put another way, it asks: which criteria usually used to validate art do such pictures fail to satisfy?

In the past some answers have been that: they do not depict the real world, as art should; or that they are not the outcome of their creators' intentions, as art should be; or that they do not communicate feelings and emotions, as true art does; or that they do not explore ideas (another function of art); or that they do not reach the heights of skill displayed by the great masters; and so on. Apart from the fact that very little art satisfies all of these criteria, each of the theories embedded in them suffers from internal inconsistencies of one sort or another (e.g. what is real about perspective?); or is in other ways not beyond reproach. Also, for each of the above criteria examples could be selected from this exhibition which would fulfil its requirements.

We are still left with a question mark, although with this kind of art (if it is art) such a situation is not novel. 'The Art of the Insane', 'Psychotic Art', 'Outsider Art', as it has been designated, has always been ambiguous and anomalous, as indeed has 'madness', 'mania', 'lunacy', 'unreason', 'mental illness', or whatever—the context in which these pictures are produced.

Because for most of its history Western art was a craft or was concerned with 'beauty', there was little scope for bizarre versions of religious images, portraits, landscapes or still-lives although there is fragmentary evidence of earlier examples of these. Apart from the obvious 'fantastic' artists, Bosch, Piero de Cosimo, Breughel, El Greco, Goya and a few others, we have to turn away from art history and towards alchemic tracts, to footnotes and marginalia for reassurance that the gods and demons, reptiles and beasts of the Celtic imagination, for example, had not been completely subdued by four centuries of classical taming.

Are we to assume that 'Psychotic Art' is a modern phenomenon? Certainly a considerable historical literature on 'madness and creativity' would lead us to expect otherwise. This topic was originally introduced by Plato who made a distinction between *divine* creative madness and *pathological* madness. His followers were not so careful. Aristotle provided an image of the melancholy artist, which was taken up in Renaissance Italy, and this was later transmuted into the unkempt genius of the Romantic era. Romanticism provided a context for the growth of the idea that an artist's personal preoccupations could be a legitimate concern of art—but the Romantic art consumer still required well painted pictures.

Art history's neglect was made good by the new science of psychology. The notion that madness and creative genius were somehow interlinked was in the nineteenth century grafted onto contemporary theories about human 'types' and later onto evolutionary theories. Unfortunately a disastrous twist with regard to the relationship between art and psycho-pathology resulted from the failure on the part of the various interested theorists to distinguish between *moral* beauty and *aesthetic* beauty; hence the equation bad art equals bad artist, degenerate art equals degenerate artist. Art history documented the ascent of man's consciousness and power and had no room for eccentrics or deviants. Psychology used psychotic art as evidence of the degeneracy of 'modern' art.

Although these notions were challenged by radical artists, it was the intensive study by psychologists and philosophers (Galton, for example), of these confused ideas about geniuses and madmen being opposite sides of the same evolutionary coin which led indirectly to the creation of the first collections of the 'art of the insane' at the end of the nineteenth century. Until the 1920s such works were regarded as curiosities; however, through the developments of Expressionism and Surrealism, through the implications for art of Freud's psychoanalysis and Jung's depth psychology, and on an individual level through the work of Hans Prinzhorn (trained in aesthetics and psychiatry), a number of artists, writers, psychologists and psychiatrists began to ponder over the weird and wonderful images now brought to their attention.

Art therapy evolved from this increased interest but with it some new aesthetic problems were introduced. For instance, it was assumed (but has not been proven) that the earlier collections were the spontaneous productions of patients. Since art therapists encourage their clients to make images, what can these have in common with the so-called spontaneous pictures? Some people were prepared to accept the latter as art, but not the former.

For psychology, all of everybody's experience must be relevant; likewise

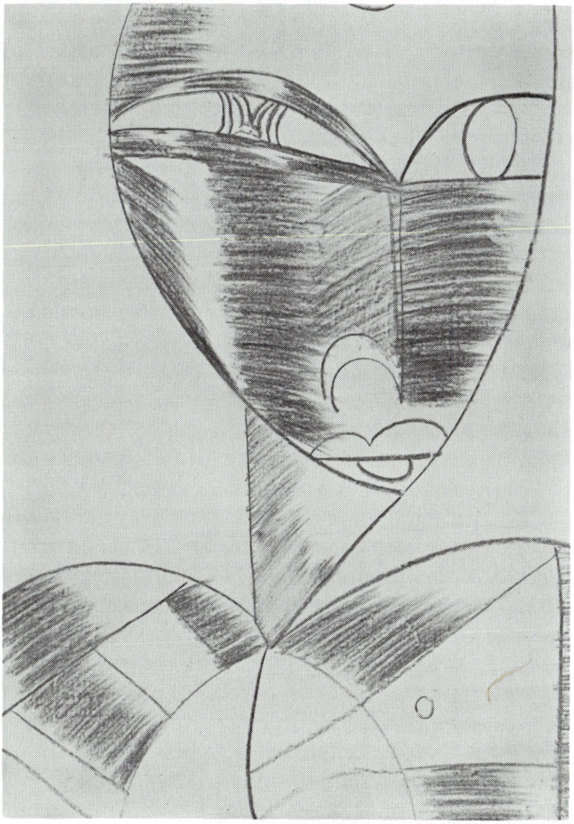

Illustration 3

for art. Perhaps it is because its rules are so difficult that artists and aestheticians frequently refuse the 'art of the insane' a place in their 'language-games'. But as Wittgenstein says: 'It is obvious that an imagined world, however different it must be from the real one, must have something, a form, in common with it' or, in other words 'We could not say what an illogical world would look like'. These are not images of illogical worlds, but their logic is obscure. In unravelling the meanings of these pictures, some of which seem only too obvious, others of which seem to defy analysis, we will certainly gain new insights into man's creative capacities. Also, if works of art are both symbols and examples of creativity, then surely these pictures, despite their anomalous position in the art world, should be included in any future history of art, both in their own right, and also as evidence of our deepening and widening understanding of art.

Art Therapy in Great Britain   Michael Edwards

As an art student during the 1950s, I had the opportunity to visit, for the first time, an art department in a hospital. The idea that patients might be involved in art was quite unknown to me. I had certainly never seen the term 'art therapy'. Thus I had no preparation for the works I was going to see; my background in art was limited to an obsession with drawing since childhood, a sense of boredom and futility in school art lessons and a strong identification with the fairly narrow aesthetic notions that were fostered in the particular art college I was attending.

The work made an immediate and lasting impression on me. What was particularly striking at the time was that the paintings seemed to represent a totally new set of values that did not correspond to art college criteria for 'good' or 'bad' work. I was used to the stylistic differences noticeable between the work of one college and another and, like most art students, I had some views about amateur and professional art. And yet the familiar aesthetic measures of appreciation seemed in this instance to be largely irrelevant. The impression was not of chaos but rather of a value system which I could not properly comprehend. The guidelines were hidden, except, it seemed, to the artists themselves and to the art therapist who worked with them. Some of the images had a shocking intensity which was expressed with clarity and precision, suggesting that there were other ways to representational skills than the process of learning to draw in which I was engaged at the time. Looking at various series of paintings by patients, it was apparent that the psychological experiences through which they were passing conditioned content, style and skill. There were some uncomfortable paradoxes—one person's work was drawn with extraordinary refinement and conviction at times when he was most ill, turning to pleasant but very ordinary little flower paintings in recovery. Other paintings were technically accomplished but somehow empty of meaning. It would be wrong, of course, to try to make generalisations from this first, highly subjective, contact with art in therapy, but for me, assumptions about art itself had been severely shaken.

Whether or not we are prepared to accept something as art is a complex and partly philosophical issue. The images in this exhibition have received some sanctioning as art simply by their presentation now in a setting known for the exhibition of distinguished works by both established and new artists. At one level, this can be seen as a simple and accepted transformation comparable with the found objects of the Dada movement; in other words, the images *are* art, simply because certain people choose to *see* them as art. This is of course far from satisfactory, or fair or respectful to the people who made the images.

The works now on public view were once almost entirely private in some sense of the word. They may have been intended only for one person besides the artist or even for the artist alone in a process of contemplation. The images are not easily or rightly seen as public communications or generalised statements. It is our privilege to be able to look at them. The messages of private art are often ambiguous, veiled or distorted and although this is also true of much public art of this century, the actual symbolic language used is often personal and idiosyncratic rather than conforming to acknowledged artistic conventions. For this reason, the work may be disturbing to preconceived notions of what art should be like. There is at least a hint too of something that can be upsetting to professional artists, the idea that psychological considerations might threaten or override artistic values. The Surrealists experimented with Freud's ideas and Abstract Expressionists acknowledged influences from psychoanalysis, but most developments in art since the growth of modern psychology have avoided its implications with what seems like determined unconsciousness. Few artists like to be told what their work 'means'.

Freud's penetrating insights cut too deeply for comfort and subsequent observations by psychoanalysts or psychiatrists which make explicit links between artistic imagery and destructive or sexual fantasies, or which find psychopathology in particular colour combinations, can impose intolerable self-conscious restrictions upon artistic freedom. Art is a language of metaphor which cannot be stripped down to a basic explanation and survive.

The influence of depth psychology on art has nevertheless been a profound one, if only through the permeating principle that one's inner life may be worthy of both attention and representation. Landscapes of the mind have become acceptable as new sources of imagery. For the non-professional artist, inner or private art may happen in one of three ways. Firstly, it may be a spontaneous happening, an impulse to represent a vision, fantasy or idea, perhaps the work of a 'primitive' living in partial isolation or a hospital patient with access to art materials. It can be argued that all art truly presents inner experience, even when it appears to mirror the real world, but there are artists whose work impresses by its strangeness and unfamiliarity, where highly personal and subjective factors seem to determine the outcome of a creative struggle with reality. Dubuffet's collection of *Art brut* and Roger Cardinal's *Outsider Art* clearly fall into this category.

Secondly, some psychotherapists have encouraged their patients to make images of dreams. Jung in particular believed that images of dreams and fantasies could be a valuable part of a healing process. Importantly, he was concerned to pay full attention to symbolic images in their own right and with the expectation of a multiplicity of meanings rather than a single explanation. This is perhaps closer to the way in which we are accustomed to approach the visual arts—by allowing associations to take place rather than by seeking to find a single hidden meaning. However, in *Modern Man in Search of a Soul* Jung wrote:

> *Although from time to time my patients produce artistically beautiful creations which might very well be shown in modern art exhibitions,*

I nevertheless treat them as wholly worthless according to the tests of serious art. It is essential that no such value be allowed them, for otherwise my patients might imagine themselves to be artists, and this would spoil the good effects of the exercise. It is not a question of art—or rather it should not be a question of art—but of something more, something other than mere art; namely the living effect upon the patient himself.

A third situation in which 'inner' art may be produced is as part of a planned therapeutic environment where art materials are freely available and an art therapist is providing encouragement, support or sympathetic non-interference. The role of an art therapist is somewhat strange, deriving from a number of influences. Both the phenomenon of spontaneously produced art in hospitals and the suggestions of making images as part of a process of psychotherapy have been important in forming a concept of therapeutic art. The writings of both Freud and Jung and more recently of the Gestalt and Existential psychologists have also been important influences. Many art therapists will be prepared to agree with Jung that they do not encourage 'art' but rather an arguably different process of involvement, seeking above all genuine spontaneity and inner truth.

What is surprising in view of this, is the fact that art therapists are almost always artists themselves. The question of training for art therapy raises both intellectual and emotional considerations and some problems of definition too, since art therapists work in settings variously administered by Departments of Health, Social Services, Education and the Home Office.

There are now three centres in Britain which offer full-time training recognised by the British Association of Art Therapists. These are at St. Albans, at Goldsmiths College in London and at Birmingham Polytechnic. All three centres are in Colleges of Art.

At both Goldsmiths and Birmingham, one-year postgraduate programmes leading to qualified art teacher status offer students the opportunity to specialise in the use of art for therapeutic purposes. This can be a main study. The St. Albans specialist course is also for one year, leading to a Diploma in Art Therapy.

There is in addition at Birmingham a Masters course which is available for qualified and experienced art therapists wishing to extend their professional understanding. At St. Albans, Rank Xerox finance a research fellow.

A year ago, the British Association of Art Therapists set up a working party, the first of its kind, to look into full-time training for art therapists. Despite some differences of emphasis between the three centres now offering full-time training, the working party has found general agreement about the outlines of a one-year post-graduate course. In broad terms these include:-

Illustration 4

1) a desirable minimum of 60 days in a practical situation, under supervision, preferably by an experienced art therapist;
2) a directed reading programme and related lecture/seminar series to include developmental psychology, psychoanalytic and related theories, psychiatry, special education for the mentally or physically handicapped or the emotionally disturbed;
3) a study programme which similarly covers a comprehensive range of specialist approaches to the use of art media for therapeutic or special educational purposes;
4) the extension of students' personal creative work;
5) provision for some kind of on-going psychodynamic experience for all students, for example through 'art therapy' orientated workshops or through psychotherapy sessions conducted by a group therapist;
6) generous tutorial contact for discussion of individual work problems, bridging between theoretical and practical elements, dealing with course assignments, etc.;
7) practice in written work, to include both case studies and some conceptual analysis.

In order to try to do justice to these constituents, one academic year is far too short a period of time. For the course to succeed it has to assume substantial previous training and/or experiences which can be regarded as relevant preparation for the actual training programme itself.

A one-year training has to reinforce elements in previous training and experience which might help to clarify art therapy objectives. Fine art students, for instance, will be likely to have encountered feelings and intuitions about their own art work which they may be prepared to acknowledge or even discuss. While many of the assumptions about personal art work may need re-examining in the new context, this examination itself can provide a useful and important ground structure upon which a more developed understanding of a functional role for art may be built.

In assuming that a satisfactory post-graduate training may reach back in this way to previous experiences, such earlier experiences have to be good enough for a meaningful and intense connection to be made. One must also be careful not to seem to suggest too literal or clumsy an approach. There is something important at risk—nothing less than the inner relationship of each individual to his or her own image-making endeavours. The quality of this internal relationship with personal creativity is a crucial determining factor in establishing sensitive and intelligent insights, intuitions and responses which make a good art therapist. This must also mean that it is as vulnerable as it is important; it would be difficult to imagine exploring this area with students—or anyone else for that matter—without a strong sense that vulnerability itself is a main dimension of such an enquiry.

Sometimes an art training may be a lonely and disappointing experience, leaving a student with a sense of depletion rather than of personal enrichment. Such disappointments can stir up feelings which ultimately lead to an interest in studying art therapy; in some cases the personal needs are too strong; the experiences in a college of art can have proved so inadequate that the student tends to project personal needs onto clients. The danger lies in the extent to which this happens and how unconscious the process is. On the other hand, the most successful therapists may be those who are really in touch with their own feelings of inadequacy—empathy is not learned from books or lectures. The therapist has to preserve a careful balance between the capacity to empathise by identifying some areas of shared feeling and the capacity to maintain enough conscious understanding for an appropriate professional role.

The training courses have consolidated their aims within the past eight years. Previously it had only been possible to train as an art teacher, or acquire some skills as an artist, as a preparation for this work. Many art therapists had no qualifications other than the temperamental ability to work in a caring role with people, combined with an attitude to art which tried to avoid imposing standards or styles. A common factor with a number of pioneer art therapists in the post-war decade was some personal experience of the relief of stress through art. The artist Adrian Hill, who wrote 'Art Versus Illness' and did much to publicise the use of art for rehabilitation in the 1940s, was himself a patient in a sanatorium for a while and it was the relief he experienced in dealing with depression and loneliness during an isolating and protracting illness that led to his encouraging others to follow his example. It could be said that the work of early art therapists like Hill was psychologically somewhat naive and yet this was an inspired amateurism which placed the healing process firmly within the boundaries of art. An early tradition was also established that art therapists were directly responsible to consultants. The work of Edward Adamson over many years at Netherne Hospital represented a close collaboration between art therapist and psychiatrists. Since in such cases the psychological or medical responsibility for treatment remains with the doctor, the role of the art therapist was essentially adjunctive. Certain kinds of artistic awareness were cultivated but this seemed to be dependent on intuition and sensitivity rather than on preconceived theoretical considerations. Such theory as there was, derived from Art Education on the one hand and Freudian and Jungian psychotherapy on the other. It is perhaps not surprising that it took so long for art therapy itself to be studied in a formal way, since the profession was established between these two considerable sources of theory, Art Education and Analytic Psychotherapy, each with an extensive literature and a range of sophisticated concepts.

There was another important influence on early developments in art therapy; a number of artists-turned-therapists themselves had undergone some personal analysis. It was through the process of analysis that the therapeutic function of art came to be validated. Theory blended with living experience and previously acquired aesthetic criteria in Art gave way at least partly, to new systems of values dependent upon feelings of personal authenticity.

An experimental therapeutic community known as the Withymead Centre was founded in Devon in 1942 by a Jungian analyst, Irene Champernowne (Champernowne) and her husband Gilbert. The Centre was concerned with psychological rehabilitation for adults and children through psychotherapy and the arts. An extremely flexible treatment programme offered workshops in painting, modelling, music and drama/movement as an adjunct to psychotherapy within a warmly supportive environment. The staff team consisted of artists, musicians and dancers on the one hand, and social workers, psychotherapists and doctors on the other, who met regularly for discussion and a genuine sharing of the therapeutic workload of the community.

Withymead established an approach to the use of the arts in therapy which has been highly influential through the many people who worked there throughout 25 years. At Withymead Jungian principles of individuation were lived out in a practical therapeutic environment.

Staff members were all qualified within their own field but 'training' at Withymead was an on-going process which was never complete; this included the opportunity for all staff to undergo training analysis, to attend and contribute to conferences and seminars held at Withymead and to share in the life of the community. The success of Withymead both as a source of psychological healing and as a training experience resulted in large measure from the imaginative vision of Irene Champernowne. Dr Anthony Stevens wrote recently of her:

> *Following Jung, she viewed the human psyche as a self-regulating mechanism capable, given appropriate circumstances, of healing itself; and she believed that in any mental illness there was a creative process at work which, provided it was assisted and understood, could enable the patient to evolve to a more satisfactory solution of his plight than the neurotic solution represented by his illness.*

Central to her thinking was the belief that 'illness' was not to be projected onto the 'patient', creating a 'them' and 'us' situation between patients and staff, but that any individual engaged in therapeutic work must be prepared to face up to and be conscious of his or her own 'ill' or less integrated aspects—throughout life. Although she regarded this as a particular responsibility for therapists, there is no doubt that she also viewed in wider terms, the lives of particularly creative individuals, as representing a similar struggle for meaning and integration, expressed and lived out through their work. Her respect for the arts in this context was such that she could take seriously any image generated by authentic feelings, from a simple naive representation to a sophisticated work of art. Furthermore this respecting of the image meant that verbalisation, explanation or interpretation could never entirely replace the original representation in its essential message. Artists, musicians, actors and dancers were plentiful in her life, as patients, colleagues and friends.

Until the end of the 1960s there were no full-time training opportunities for art therapists. The British Association of Art Therapists originally decided to approach the problems of training and improved professional status through identifying art therapists as specialised members of the art teaching profession, partly because the Government Department of Education seemed more promising for negotiation purposes than the Department of Health, and also perhaps because the 'educational' model rather than the 'treatment' model seemed more suited to the way in which art therapy had emerged in Britain.

There was—and still is— a strong emphasis on art itself, a recognition that through a deep experience in art one may be able to help others to become involved and be helped *by* becoming involved. And just as a training in art for the art therapist seemed to imply an educational rather than a medical background so it also seemed that psychotherapy, play therapy and art therapy (or sometimes 'remedial art education') were more likely to be found—and promoted—in the special school or child guidance centre rather than the hospital.

A further influence which may have encouraged early art therapists to think of themselves as special art teachers was from art education itself. The writings of Herbert Read had dominated and sometimes inspired much art teaching of the post-war period and it can be argued that the stated aims of art teaching and art therapy were closely related for as long as art education in Britain was under the influence of Read's ideas, incorporating as they did a rationale for art teaching derived, somewhat tenuously, from both Freud and Jung.

Read's influence declined as 'self-expression' became something of a stereotype, and the way was prepared for the 'basic design' experiments which followed in the Colleges of Art.

If art therapists felt they had some support from educational quarters, they had reason to feel disillusioned by the lack of response from the medical side. Salaries were about half those paid by educational authorities and the earlier interest shown by the medical profession dwindled away so that art therapy departments in hospitals, if they survived, tended to become isolated from the parent institution.

Thus 'art therapy' as part of a full-time training first appeared as an optional specialisation at several centres, all in colleges of art, which offered post-graduate art teacher courses. Meanwhile at St. Albans an experimental pilot course, intended mainly for occupational therapists and nurses led to the establishment of a full-time training leading to a 'Certificate in Remedial Art'. This has now developed into the present Art Therapy Diploma course.

It would seem a fair generalisation to say that there has been a recent tendency for the training work of the three centres to move to a more central position. This has resulted partly from the constructive discussion within the B.A.A.T. working party and the consequent overview of the whole training question. The courses have all become less theoretical and more dynamic in structure, giving a good deal of importance to the quality of involvement of each art therapy student. The two art education programmes seem to be moving in the direction of a more distinct identity for each of the roles, therapist and teacher, using the distinction in order to delineate more sharply the responsibilities and goals inherent in each task.

It is still something of an open question that there may be advantages and disadvantages in assuming that the discipline of art therapy can be learnt with a broad and more general context. As far as employment is concerned, the tendency seems to be for increased job opportunities which demand some kind of hybrid training, blending, in varying proportions, the skills of artist, therapist and teacher. What matters of course is that this should not lead to an unacceptable dilution of the essential skills. The art therapist's work demands willingness not to interfere, a feeling for intensity, for recognising the projective power contained within symbolic material, and an understanding of the consequent protective shield that has to be provided around the image-making process.

Illustration 5

The Use of Therapeutic Art in Child Guidance

Diana Halliday

For a number of years, I have worked with children in Child Guidance Centres, using art as the main medium of communication.

In *Playing and Reality*, Dr. Donald Winnicot describes what we do together. 'Psychotherapy', he says, 'takes place in the overlap of two areas of playing, that of the patient and that of the therapist. Psychotherapy has to do with two people playing together.' Further on, he adds, 'Playing facilitates growth and therefore health; playing leads into group relationships.' Stressing the universality of play, he observes that it is 'just as evident in the analyses of adults as it is in the case of our work with children.'

Both playing and painting are spontaneous, creative activities. Both have an element of magic, the more potent in art since the end-product is visible, tangible, lasting. Both process and product are revealing and have the important advantage that they provide evidence of feelings and states of mind as well as a permanent record of development, growth and change. Whether from a series of squiggles or of paintings, the themes that emerge are of the utmost significance to both patient and therapist. The child's feelings and fantasies undergo a process of transformation in the doing, and this is an integrative function of art therapy. (I am thinking of a girl who, feeling angry and bad, painted a huge spider in her landscape. Then, as she felt first relieved and then exultant, she covered up the spider and painted an enormous sun on top of it, making the rays out of drinking straws for extra emphasis. These unconscious feelings, expressed symbolically, could not have been put into words. There seemed no need to block her spontaneity by interpreting at the time.) Art therapists must allow intuition and experience to tell them when (or whether) to discuss the work. Sensitivity to the individual is the guiding factor in the delicate balance of a relationship. Not only painting and modelling but all the arts are generated in the freedom of self-expression, which grows with time and trust.

The art therapist's role has been defined as that of an active/passive participant/observer. I see myself as a partner, closely involved in my child's unconscious mind and feelings, sharing his inner world to the extent of my ability—and his willingness. Together, we can perhaps eventually heal some of the hurts.

How do children come for treatment to a Child Guidance Centre? Parents, head teachers, doctors and the Social Services may request treatment; and children may refer themselves. In fact, a fifteen year old girl once came to the clinic (she had been a patient at the age of nine) ostensibly for advice on the choice of an art school, but actually to seek help in controlling her temper. They may have educational difficulties, neurotic and behavioural disorders, psychosomatic conditions or more severe psychiatric problems. Some receive remedial teaching; those more likely to benefit from art therapy would be referred to me.

Children are referred right through school age. My youngest patient was Tina, a bright-eyed four year old. One of a pair of twins, her sister had been brain-damaged at birth and was not expected to live long. A normal, happy little girl at school, Tina betrayed anxiety at home. She frequently identified with her 'baby' sister and demanded the same treatment. She told the Health Visitor one day that there was a monster in the garden who ate babies. In the hope that she would work out her fears and fantasies, she was referred for therapy. The first time she came she darted round the room like a trapped bird, both frightened and yet eager to play with the toys; her mother was present. On the second visit she let her mother go without difficulty and, after some play, she picked up a lump of clay and modelled what she told me was a monster. Her anxiety must have been aroused by her creation; her mother reported that she had screamed and screamed before the next visit and she never came back.

Drawing and painting come as naturally as singing, dancing and playing and all of these are generated spontaneously within the one-to-one session at the clinic. There is always an element of shared surprise and delight at these manifestations of creativity. I remember a ten year old girl suddenly acting a 'Ruth Draper' type of three-act play, making it up as she went along and dramatising life at home with her mother and father. The Wendy House provided the setting and is in fact the scene of fantasy, comedy and tragedy, wherein boys and girls express their unconscious feelings. What has been called the 'ecology' of the therapy room includes a vast range of equipment, sand, water, punchballs, games and toys, of which art materials are the most important part. All of them enable aggression, regression, destructiveness and reconstruction to be worked through. The blackboard may be the child's universe, outer-space, a wall for graffiti or even a place of learning—where the child teaches me, as often as not. The typewriter is one of the most subtle instruments of communication (however maltreated it may be), and I equate it with art in its creative power; it provides a link between visual and verbal communication, between patient and therapist. As, for instance, in the case of Ronnie, depressed, fearful on his first visit to the therapist. He looked longingly at the typewriter, so I typed 'Dear Ronnie, I like you very much. My name is Mrs. Halliday.' Quick as a flash, he typed back: 'it like yoy to. what can we do. can do somewaing now i can write it.'

Others typed dreams, poems, hymns of love or hate, imaginary letters to employers, to lawyers, expressing anxiety about jobs—or about parents separating. Andy (aged 10) typed a libretto for the opera he was writing. Articulate and intelligent, he was undersized, having been outgrown by his siblings. He took refuge in a fantasy world in which he was the great actor (hero and villain—the polarities within himself), the great composer, the great playwright. Coming to the clinic was for him a serious business. He denied knowledge of any problems but carefully saved up his dreams and painted them. A passionate little boy, overwhelmed by the violence of his repressed anger, he derived satisfaction from the freedom to express these in the presence of the therapist, but it was many months before he could trust her enough to risk playing. At home everything in his life was organised for him. While resenting the discipline he could only 'let go' in art; that was earnest—playing was frivolous, childish.

Danny had witnessed violence at an early age. His mother's marriage broke up after her husband had assaulted her when she was pregnant. Father had married again and had a new family. Mother had re-married, this time to an alcoholic and this marriage too had come to an end. Dan was isolated, bitter, full of unarticulated misery and resentment, which he worked out in violent play at the clinic. Play was destructive, but his art was the opposite. In paint, clay, balsawood, he made his own world. He created a three-dimensional landscape for a tramp to roam in and stuck pieces of balsawood together to make a house for himself. This construction gave him deep satisfaction. He named it 'The House of the Future'. At the end of treatment, Dan built a balsawood station, 'The Terminus'. Then he both typed and wrote on the blackboard: 'I am the King'. He was becoming 'His Own Man', though his problems were far from resolved.

Balsawood also served to make a dramatic finale for David. Now nine, he had been attending the clinic for over a year. He was unable to talk about his feelings but symbolised them on the last visit, by making a cross with his full name on it and planting it on top of a sandy grave. I followed this sadly, feeling he had buried the self we had both known. That self was the child whose secret world I had shared each week. David the man was born five minutes later: quickly he wrote his name, in bold capitals, on a larger strip of balsa and affixed it to the door of the Wendy House. He shut himself up in it (excluding me) and typed away busily. I wondered what fantasy he was enacting, when he called me in and whispered (as he jammed all the keys together) 'These are all the boys at school crowding outside the canteen door, waiting for dinner; and this is me' (pressing hard on the top row of keys), 'I'll be first in!' Some of his hunger had in fact been satisfied during our time together, but he was far from sated. It was David's mother who had benefited from the one session in family art therapy we had managed to do. Following to some extent the procedure described by Hania Kwiatkowska, who teaches and practises family art therapy in Washington, D.C., the family did a joint painting. His mother declared later that she had obtained more insight into the family's interactions than she had believed possible. I believe that family art therapy has an important contribution to make to psychotherapy with children, and can shorten the time otherwise required.

The knowledge that, for one hour a week, the child is the sole concern of 'his' therapist and that he is accepted and valued for his unique self—both good and bad—is fundamental to healing. We are on a journey together, a journey of discovery, the uncharted sea being perhaps the unknown, unidentified parts of himself. With creative energy we cement the hurt and damaged self, with the bricks and mortar of love, paint and clay and hope eventually to integrate the inner and outer worlds.

Self-awareness and self-regard come about through 'doing'. Physically, a painting can grow proportionately with the child's need to externalise his vision. To this end sheets of paper, or a continuous roll can be used. The fifteen year old girl to whom I referred earlier had never forgotten the vast 'canvas' she had covered in painting her volcano. There is an importance in letting the child extend his fantasy world on this scale. Apart from anything else, the sense of achievement and wonder at what he has produced is good in itself.

Lee (aged 6) was a pathetic little fellow, miserable and insecure when he began treatment. He was faced with probably uprooting from his home and friends. The upheaval of a transatlantic move was added to the uncertainty about which parent he would be living with. All this anxiety was expressed by making maps and charts—both psychic and geographic—of travel by ship, train and plane. These developed spontaneously into scroll paintings. Lee felt his future was at stake and he knew how urgent it was to describe graphically what could not be put into words. Eventually he was able to adjust to the changes happily.

Developing trust takes time, and healing is a slow process which cannot be rushed. It can be undermined or blocked by the impatience or mistrust of uneasy parents. Wanting to know 'what goes on' in the session, they may question the child or, at a crucial moment in therapy, will ask him how much longer it has to go on. (Often the children themselves know when they are ready to leave, when learning becomes more important than attending the clinic). Play, to some families, seems a waste of time. One day Alan, who had been in terrible trouble, asked if he might bring his grandmother up to the therapy room. She watched him playing and painting and then commented sarcastically: 'No wonder he likes coming here'. Then, unable to restrain herself, she hissed, 'And when does the lady smack your bottom?' 'She doesn't', came the terse reply. But he was not allowed to come back.

The dehumanising effect of uniforms—and helmets— is often demonstrated in play and painting. Putting on a policeman's helmet, Andy, aged 8, but behaving like a four year old because his violent feelings must be concealed, lisps: 'I want to be a policeman when I grow up. I will be allowed to kill and get paid for it as well'. More seriously, Eric (9) painted armed warriors, their faces covered with armour. He showed no feeling

Illustration 6

and could neither play nor talk about himself. His early history was one of emotional deprivation. His father had opted out and his mother was over-burdened with the care of a large family. Eric was neglected and became a loner. Several years later, he has been accused of murdering an old man. This is not to say that all children who paint soldiers are potential murderers, but such paintings do provide clues to their feelings. They need to work through these and understand them. The harm done in early childhood might be too great to be counteracted at a later stage or perhaps the help available may be inadequate to his needs. Violence in young boys and girls originates mostly, I believe, in the violence done to them, whether it be by the parents or society. I am reminded of a twelve year old boy, deemed autistic, with whom I worked for a year or two. When he came in, he would ask me to open my mouth. He would touch it gently and inspect my teeth. Then we would have long periods of 'eye contact'; the game would be who could outstare the other. I'm afraid it took me time to realise that this child, who had been rejected from birth by his mother, was putting me in her place and living the experience he had never had of seeing himself in her eyes and of getting to know her by feel. At first his reaction to my touch had been to punch me. The day 'treatment' ended, I should not have been surprised by the little note he left behind: 'Mrs. Halliday is my best friend and I love her'.

His art work was typical of many autistic children—hundreds of repetitive chessmen, rockets, planes, perfect clay models of prehistoric animals—but what had really happened in the clinic was that Andrew looked into my eyes as if I were a mirror . . . he experienced himself, as the small baby does reflected in his mother's gaze. This was art therapy.

Illustration 7

Art and Psychopathology: a history of its Study and Applications

John Henzell

The use of image-making for psychiatric purposes known as art therapy, which has given rise to most of the pictures in this exhibition, is of relatively recent origin. It first appeared in the late 1930s and developed chiefly in English-speaking countries, in Britain and North America. Its antecedents, however, go back to the beginning of psychiatry as we know it, to those years in the late 18th and early 19th centuries when madness ceased to be explained in terms of demonic possession or an imbalance of humours but rather as a manifestation of pathology by analogy with physical illness. Thus what had hitherto been seen as a disorder of the imagination came to be thought of instead as a disorder of the brain. Nevertheless, treatments which purported to cure this metaphorical malady by acting on it through the body did not assume a tangible form in psychiatric practice immediately. The physicians who first treated insanity did so by various means of persuasion, example and exhortation. Elaborate forms of representation were devised in order to convince patients of the error of their delusional beliefs; such representations often took the form of dramatic charades performed by asylum attendants, or of exemplary reflections in strategically placed mirrors. Yet representation was a technique available to both patient and physician and it could be employed in a graphic form.

The first publication showing a drawing by a psychiatric patient appeared in 1810, a doubly unique event in that it was also the first book devoted to a single psychiatric case. Its author, John Haslam, was a physician at the Bethlem Hospital, then perhaps better known as Bedlam. This work, *Illustrations of Madness*, dealt with the case of James Tilley Matthews who spent between 1798 and 1813 as a patient at the hospital. The published drawing, one of a number of designs by Matthews, depicts the operation of what he referred to as an 'air loom', a pneumatic machine by means of which his imagined enemies assailed him and caused the appalling sensations which characterised his affliction. Matthews and Haslam intended the drawing to be an illustration of mutually opposed arguments. Matthews intended his design to demonstrate the reasonableness of his beliefs, it served as ostensive evidence:

> *It is with Me a Great Object to have them delivered up to Me alive and in their Perfect Senses, And to have their Apparatus unbroken Very whole and in the state they used, with their Modes etc. Publickly Exhibited.*

To Haslam, on the other hand, publication of the drawing provided evidence in a contrary direction: it counted amongst the reasons for assuming Matthews to be insane. It was, so to speak, an involuntary confession.

From the outset art and image-making seen in the context of psychopathology have served the purpose of expressing or substantiating a point of view, that of the patient and that of the physician. Naturally it is the psychiatrist, psychologist, psychotherapist or art therapist who has generally had access to the means by which opinions are made public; the patient's view has for the most part remained embodied in his images.

After Haslam nothing appeared in print concerning this subject for over half a century. Even when well known artists such as Richard Dadd went mad little attention was paid to their artistic development subsequent to their admission to an asylum. They were placed 'beyond the pale' and such interest as did exist in their art was in the main a concern with their past sanity rather than with their current lack of it. In spite of this neglect certain psychiatrists built up collections of patients' spontaneously produced images. These often co-existed with other curiosities of contemporary lunatic asylums: carvings, sculpture made from kneaded bread, escape tools, casts of abnormal bodily parts, and other mementoes of madness. By the end of the century a few psychiatrists had written about such pictorial work—Simon and Tardieu, for example, discussed possible diagnostic applications in forensic medicine. For the most part, though, few investigations of this material were carried out.

The most notable exception was the work of Cesare Lombroso of the University of Turin, who had probably assembled the largest collection of mental patients' art works of his day. In his famous study of genius and insanity Lombroso proposed an identity between the two states. He attempted to demonstrate this by means of quasi-statistical arguments, by interminable comparisons of biographical, anecdotal, behavioural, and anatomical details as well as by a study of the art of the insane. Curious as Lombroso's approach may seem today he exerted considerable influence at the time. There were, however, other developments taking place which were to have a far more profound bearing on our subject.

Firstly Sigmund Freud's investigations of mental processes were to culminate in the methods and theories of psychoanalysis. Freud set out to illuminate abnormal psychological functioning by deriving psychopathology from a more general theory of the mind. The psychic mechanisms he studied in order to further and illustrate his investigations—dreams, slips of the tongue, forgetting, jokes, and erotic fantasies—were everyday mental phenomena common to all men. It required only a small step to apply the same exploratory methods to art. From time to time these new ideas were applied to art if not to the actual image-making of psychiatric patients (in particular we have Freud's studies of Michelangelo and Leonardo da Vinci). This arose in part from the need to use the 'case study' as a means of demonstrating psychoanalytic theory. Considerations of confidentiality prevented analysts from making as much use as they would have wished of their own patients' case material so they turned instead to the hypothetical and retrospective analysis, or

'pathography', of historical characters of whom considerable biographical detail, often in the form of their art, was available.
Secondly, an increasing number of artists and critics had cast the most serious doubts on the rigid standards of late 19th century academicism in the visual arts. Alternative aesthetic paradigms were sought including the art forms and techniques of other cultures. Parallel to the technical and aesthetic innovations brought about as a consequence there were commensurate and equally important evocations of new psychological attitudes. Blake saw the imagination as the source of all that was real; Gauguin was pleased to call his attempt to recapture a lost and primitive innocence through painting 'barbaric'; the group of artists dubbed the 'fauves' or 'wild beasts' by a hostile critic willingly adopted this epithet themselves. There had in addition been the recognition, at least amongst a small circle of artists and intellectuals, of the talents of two painters of which a serious consideration would have been impossible previously: of Van Gogh who vividly illustrated that artistic genius and extreme mental instability could exist in the same person, and of Henri Rousseau (le Douanier) whose naive but nobly designed paintings demonstrated the heights that could be attained by an untutored artist. Later, while Kandinsky, Malevich and Mondrian were abandoning figuration altogether, Paul Klee cultivated the technical devices of children and 'primitives' in his most sophisticated art. Indeed, in 1907 Marcel Réja had noted the similarities between the art of the mad and that of children and primitives. Thus states of mind alternative to and sometimes, as in the case of the Dadaists, opposed to what Charcot had called the 'official consciousness', were increasingly explored by artists and writers no less than by Freud and the psychoanalysts.

Yet if the connections between contemporary art and psychoanalysis remained latent at this time, the full significance of 'le Douanier' Rousseau was equally hidden. He was certainly appreciated by some as a painter but the truth he embodied as a person was hardly understood before 1920. He was deemed to be a freak of nature, an extraordinary and novel exception, or even a practical joke. There was little suspicion, except amongst a handful of unusually cultured and perceptive psychiatrists, that there might be many others like Rousseau manufacturing their strange and idiosyncratic images both inside and out of institutions for the insane.

In 1921 the Swiss psychiatrist Walter Morgenthaler published a study concerning Adolf Wölfli, a schizophrenic and prolific artist and writer. Morgenthaler's attitude to his subject was quite novel in that he focused as much on Wölfli the artist as on Wölfli the madman. Unlike other psychiatric writers he disclosed the name of his subject and included photographs of Wölfli in the book. Morgenthaler argued that Wölfli's art was a spontaneous attempt to attain psychological equilibrium and that it therefore served a curative function. In this conclusion he anticipates later writers such as Karl Jaspers and Anna Freud.

Undoubtedly the major figure at this time was Hans Prinzhorn whose *Bildnerei der Geisteskranken* (Artistry of the Mentally Ill) appeared in 1922, a book unprecedented in its scope and depth and which has remained a classic in its field ever since. In 1918 Prinzhorn took up an appointment at the Heidelberg Psychiatric Clinic where he was encouraged by the director, Karl Wilmanns, to extend a collection of patients' art works and to carry out an investigation of this material. In three years Prinzhorn amassed over 5,000 examples of such image-making culled from asylums, hospitals and clinics throughout Europe. He was a man of singularly wide culture and intellectual attainment. An art historian, aesthetician, musician, as well as a psychiatrist, he knew many of the leading artistic and intellectual figures of his day and was closely associated with the Blaue Reiter group. He was fully aware of the most recent advances in psychiatry and psychology, in particular the new psychiatry of Bleuler and the innovatory theories of the psychoanalysts and of the Gestalt psychologists. In approaching his investigation Prinzhorn assumed that artistic activity was a manifestation of a 'configurative urge', that visual art was the permanent trace of 'gestural expression', and that this mode of expression communicated itself directly without the intervention of any intellectual or verbal apparatus. Struck by the power and expressive force of the images he had collected he concluded that the level of the psyche from which such activity proceeded was sufficiently fundamental and deep to be relatively unaffected by a psychotic process. In fact, by its disruption of culturally imposed checks and inhibitions, a psychosis may encourage the release of artistic expression. He noted in particular the way in which his patients' work often strikingly resembled the art forms and images of other cultures, and here he implicitly supports the theories of C. G. Jung. Most interestingly of all he thought the general emotional attitudes evinced by his schizophrenic artists and by much contemporary art were remarkably similar. Prinzhorn followed the example of Morgenthaler in giving the identities of the subjects of his book and was the first to place the work of psychotic artists in a clear perspective.

Although unparalleled in its scale Prinzhorn's investigation was not an isolated phenomenon—further aspects of art and psychopathology began to receive attention from this time onwards. In 1920 Oskar Pfister, a Freudian analyst, published a study of expressionism in art; his aesthetic concepts were somewhat idiosyncratic, sharing the awkwardness of much early psychoanalytic writing about art. Those analysts who applied their theories to art directly did so by way of interpretations of the unconscious symbols concealed in the ostensible subject matter of the images they studied. It was exactly this kind of approach which so repelled many artists and critics like the formalist Roger Fry. During this period psychoanalytic writing contained more of interest concerning the visual arts when dealing with other matters than with the subject itself.

The issue of diagnosis has remained crucial for any approach made by institutional psychiatry to the image-making of the mentally ill. Paradoxically, Prinzhorn's book inspired a long succession of studies in which the art works of psychiatric patients were examined from the point of view of symptomatology in spite of the fact that he doubted the feasibility of such a procedure. Such classificatory investigations were intended to reveal signs of a pathology on the basis of which a medical opinion could be ventured or sustained, as if the graphic image could be a kind of psychiatric equivalent of the X-ray plate in radiography. A diagnostic emphasis is also to be seen in the 'projective test'. In the early 1920s Hermann Rorschach devised and elaborated what has become the best-known of all such techniques, the 'ink-blot' test. Projective techniques are an application of the psychoanalytic theory of 'projection', a means by which a person conceals wishes and desires from himself by attributing them to some aspect of the external world. Other tests followed Rorschach's, sometimes including a greater degree of figuration in the stimulus image, and still later diagnostic opinions were derived from the patient's drawings as in Karen Machover's 'Draw a Person Test'.

In contrast to such clinical procedures a few psychoanalysts encouraged their patients to draw and paint for the sake of the material this made available to the analysis. The use of such images might be compared to the interpretation of the patient's dreams in analytic therapy. Jung's fascination with the spontaneous productions of psychotic patients led to an interest amongst his followers in the symbolic significance of man's images which was reflected in their psychotherapeutic technique. A patient's paintings and drawings might reveal deep unconscious psychic activity and therefore make this otherwise concealed mental substratum perceptible.

Such techniques anticipate art therapy. In fact by 1940 one might say that it existed in all but name. Before describing the advent and growth of art therapy as an identifiable discipline I would like briefly to indicate two other developments from which art therapy, perhaps rather to its cost, has remained distant.

In 1945 Jean Dubuffet commenced his collection of *art brut*. His object was to seek out that image-making which had eluded cultural conditioning and processing, which was, so to speak, in a pure and raw state. He felt that art and thought alike were renewed and sustained by these 'scraps' of culture. He included the art of the mad in his concept of *art brut* and collected and exhibited many examples of psychotic art. Both he and Prinzhorn shared an interest in art existing in such a pure condition and both have been instrumental in bringing the work of insane artists before a wider than purely psychiatric public. After the war André Breton collaborated with Dubuffet in forming the *Compagnie de l'art brut*. Breton had a longstanding interest in psychiatric matters and his correspondence with Freud is only one instance of the attraction that psychoanalysis had always held for the Surrealists. Others have asserted that mad art is an exemplar of all art. Leo Navratil has drawn attention to the creativity of schizophrenia while Arnulf Rainer and Ernst Fuchs have argued that, far from treating madness, we should consider it an ultimate form of sanity and set up institutes of insane culture where forms of psychotic expression could be encouraged. Navratil's ideas recall those of the philospher and psychiatrist Karl Jaspers, like Prinzhorn a protégé of Wilmanns, who advanced the notion of 'creative illness'. Jaspers thought that madness might be the wreckage of psychic residue brought about by an overwhelming creative and mystical experience.

Important developments in psychoanalytic theory begun by Freud himself in the 1920s and continuing in their different ways in the work of Anna Freud and Melanie Klein, led to a transformation in psychoanalytic approaches to art and to aesthetics. Anna Freud's concept of creative activity as an 'ego defence' against the threat of an impending psychotic upheaval, a reversal of Jaspers' surmise, and the Kleinian theory of 'object relations' have facilitated approaches to the structure of art. Since the Second World War a number of writers have applied these theories, or admixtures of them with aesthetic concepts, to the visual arts. If such writing has not often dealt directly with the productions of psychiatric patients or with art therapy, it has suggested a number of intriguing theoretical vantage points. Some of those involved in this reappraisal have been analysts, such as Ernst Kris, Hanna Segal and Marion Milner, while others like Adrian Stokes, Anton Ehrenzweig and Richard Wollheim have been aestheticians.

The first art therapists appeared just before and during the Second World War. Arthur Segal and Adrian Hill in England and Margaret Naumberg in America were the early pioneers. In many ways their respective approaches typify different emphases in art therapy which still exist today. Naumberg's theory of art therapy developed from her work with children and is firmly based on the psychoanalytic model. The art therapist functions as a therapist in his or her own right interpreting the 'symbolic speech' of the patient's images. This professional and clinical style is characteristic of art therapy in the United States. Segal was a painter who, through his associations with the Blaue Reiter group, had known Prinzhorn. He left Germany in 1936 and set up his School of Painting in London where he taught artists as well as psychiatrists and their patients. He believed art possessed therapeutic properties; the laws of psychological functioning and of art were linked and therefore a valid art experience, that is one in conformity with the laws of art, was highly integrative. In 1941 his school moved to Oxford, where servicemen were encouraged to attend his classes, remaining there until his death in 1944. Subsequently his school returned to London where his daughter has continued to run it along the lines he instituted. Some of the first English art therapists attended Segal's school. He thought of himself more as a teacher than a therapist and one can see connections between his work and that of educationalists like Franz Cizek. Hill began to use art therapy in a hospital for chest and tuberculosis patients during the war. His type of art therapy was mainly recreational and its therapeutic aspects arose as effects of the art activity of the patient.

One might say that Naumberg's model of art therapy stresses therapy while the more distinctly English models of Segal and Hill depend on the art aspect. Further distinctions can be drawn: American art therapists have been almost aggressively professional in their creation of a psychiatric practice whereas their British colleagues are imbued more with a sense of enthusiastic amateurism. Hence the profusion of American writing in the field and the relative dearth of it in England, and in consequence the considerable reputation of a pioneer like Naumberg and the obscurity of Segal. Of course the contrast is not as simple as this. Art therapy in both countries has become more eclectic as it has developed. During the 1950s in this country a number of art therapists, such as Edward Adamson, adapted their practice to large psychiatric institutions while the interest in the symbolism of the unconscious of Irene Champernowne, the Jungian psychotherapist, and her artist colleagues has had its effect on art therapy. In the United States Edith Kramer argued that the aesthetic quality of images made by patients in therapy, the richness of the art experience, was too often neglected. A simple lineage from early models is further complicated by the more recent popularity in art therapy of techniques deriving from 'humanistic' psychology, encounter groups and Gestalt therapy; and the emphasis on therapeutic groups rather than the individual client or patient has increasingly pervaded all kinds of psychiatric practice on both sides of the Atlantic. More recently still, British and American art therapists have set up professional organisations and created courses of training. What, little more than thirty years ago, was the work of a few inspired pioneers has now become an accepted professional discipline.

Yet the pragmatism required in obtaining a necessary professional recognition has perhaps led art therapy into a somewhat contradictory position, a situation which has often forced its practitioners to choose between the art or therapy aspects of their craft. To some extent I think one may discern this alternating emphasis in this exhibition. A rationale for art therapy can hardly appeal to physical causality in the manner in which the medical model underlying most psychiatry does. Hence the first art therapists were caught in the same dilemma that had faced analysts and psychotherapists in attempting to reach a *modus vivendi* with institutional psychiatry. As a result they tended to adopt one of two courses of action: they stressed the clinical side of their work, adapting current theory to this end, and here there is a connection between pragmatism and a certain theoretical conservatism; or they minimised their therapeutic responsibility and concentrated on the art ingredient

of their practice so as not to conflict with their psychiatric patrons.
Art therapy should now be sufficiently established to allow the reassessment of its theoretical and experimental base in the light of contemporary developments in psychology, aesthetics, psychoanalysis, and the other disciplines which impinge on it. Given this, art therapy will be able fully to realise its exciting potential and bequeath new insights to our human understanding. It is to be hoped that this timely exhibition will act as a stimulus in this direction.

Illustration 8 Stanley LENCH

Catalogue

Work is individually labelled in the exhibition. It was thought pointless to duplicate this information here without adequate illustration of the work itself. Notes have been given for all works illustrated in the Catalogue. This section comprises statements made by art therapists who have submitted notes about their aims and working methods. The list is arranged alphabetically according to the name of the hospital.

The Adamson Collection, London

These paintings from Netherne Hospital have been selected from a collection of seventy thousand which I have assembled during the past thirty-five years. They are not intended to be works of art, and they are hardly ever the work of artists, but they often have a rare incidental quality of beauty. These pictures are merely documents which record changes in the labyrinth world of a mental patient's mind. Mental illness often heightens artistic perception, but as it can never replace it, it would be wrong to suggest that all these pictures have a direct relationship to the work of practising painters, indeed, artist painters often discriminate between their paintings and their psychiatric illusions. Art therapy is not simply a means to distract the patient; it gives him an interest but goes further in that it provides additional aids to recovery for the patient, and also helps the psychiatrist in the diagnosis and treatment of the illness.

Edward Adamson is consultant art therapist at the Netherne Hospital, Coulsdon, Surrey, Hertfordshire College of Art and Design, St. Albans and Roehampton Institute of Higher Education.

Barrow Hospital, Bristol

Art Therapist: Roy Thornton

My first aim is to help the patient to work through his immediate problems and ultimately to help him to achieve harmony and to understand himself. In this way my role is that of guide, helping the patient to acquire tools of insight—to develop intuition—to use creativity as a source of motivation within himself. As well as individual meetings, I do groups in which art is a vital source of psychotherapy material, with which I use mainly Gestalt Therapy and sometimes Transactional analysis techniques.

Video is now used as a means to increase patients' awareness of themselves and for them to gain some insight into how they appear to others. I am concerned that patients work together in this, operating the equipment and discussing what they have made.

Bexley Hospital, Kent

Art Therapist: Britta Warsi

I see my role as essentially that of an analyst or an activating agent and that of art therapy as a therapeutic effort to promote unity in a fragmented self. It is my deeply held conviction that creativity and therapy are inextricably united being derived from a basic universal human need to expand our feelings and to experience a growing self-awareness.

Bridgwater Day Hospital, Bridgwater

Art Therapist: David Bostock (also art therapist at Tone Vale Hospital, Taunton 1974-6).

Spontaneous painting and modelling from the imagination can play an important part in the process of healing. The creative process is ultimately a mystery yet it need not be fully understood to be utilised as a force of natural wisdom and healing potential existing within the individual. My role as an art therapist is to create the atmosphere of safety and freedom necessary for this process to take place. People are encouraged and helped to express themselves as spontaneously as possible and to experience the products of their imagination.

Interpretation in my view is not essential. Ultimately it is only via the senses and those intuitive faculties of the mind which are far older than words that we can hope to understand. If interpretations are made it is important they are made by the creators of the work themselves. By working in this way people can contact the unknown or unconscious within themselves and discover their hidden potentialities and re-vitalising forces. Images symbolic of the depths of the individual's inner self are externalised and explored in the light of consciousness. The therapeutic potential of this activity can vary from a form of exorcism to a source of integration and psychological growth.

Byrne Collection, Matlock

This collection was assembled by Peter Byrne while doing research into art therapy. They were collected mostly from discarded material at the Maudsley Hospital, London. As this hospital has no art therapy department it is probable that most of the works were spontaneously produced.

Ealing Child Guidance Centre

Art Therapist: Diana Halliday

Loving art and loving children, it seems natural to use the one to help the other.
In art therapy (a paramedical profession), one's deep concerns combine to form a whole; both a way of being and a way of life. Engendering the healing powers of creative art, it also opens up a vast and ever growing realm of visual communication; practice and research go hand in hand. Understanding this non-verbal language is the other part of therapy, through which the patient discovers what his feelings are, the meaning of his fantasies and can come eventually to integrate his inner and his outer worlds. This process leads to maturation, autonomy and change. My role is that of helper or co-worker; we build on a relationship of mutual trust. The child sees himself reflected both in his art work and in my eyes and gets (one hopes) to recognise himself.
I believe (with Eric Gill) that 'the artist is not a special kind of man: every man is a special kind of artist!' and that art is therapy for one and all, of any age, in sickness or in health.

Friern Hospital, Barnet, London

Art Therapist: Christine Walker 1967-1975

In an art therapy department one needs materials that are easy to use. All the departments I have worked in have had a wide variety of general art materials. It is important that the patient has the best opportunity to exercise his own inventiveness and judgement. Materials that are too specific tend to trap the patient into a particular technique or craft—therefore a whole cupboard full of different (and inexpensive) kinds of paper and card can be better than a ream of watercolour paper. Household paint and powder colour and coloured inks allow wider possibilities than a box of artist's oils.
So too the skill of the art therapist lies in offering oneself in an undogmatic way so as to catch the imagination of the patient without confusing it. Of course, there has to be a theoretical structure behind one's work, but over time I have come to believe that it does not matter particularly which. While one's opinions influence oneself and one's work they should not overrule what the patient can say for himself. We should be like our materials—involving, exciting and easy to use.

Fulbourne Hospital, Cambridge

Art Therapist: Tessa Dalley

The essence of art in therapy is communication. Painting can transmit profound emotional experiences from one person to many. Through the process of creative expression inner feelings, thoughts and problems are brought to the surface and shared. Once externalised in this way, barriers surrounding all of us are removed. Art provides a powerful means to mirror the process of change in a personal crisis and at the same time fosters an ability to work through problems in a more positive way for both individuals and a group in therapy.

Glenside Hospital, Bristol

Art Therapists: Michael Donnelly
Suzanne Charlton

Art therapy as we see it provides therapy as part of the clinical team approach within the hospital. It provides a range of possibilities for both groups and individual clients, whether in-patients or out-patients. We feel that the therapist's role is to help to guide clients to a better understanding of themselves and their productions. Sometimes the therapist takes an active role in the process by providing goals creating structures and acting as a catalyst. It is always our aim to place value on the individual and to encourage personal growth.

Guttmann Maclay Collection

Institute of Psychiatry, University of London

This collection was started in the 1930s by Dr W. Maclay and Dr E. Guttmann, two consultant psychiatrists at the Maudsley Hospital, London. It was assembled with the specific view of comparing changes in work made by artists during 'normal' health with that made during periods of mental instability. Changes in the perception of artists is also recorded in a series of works made under the influence of Mescalin, a hallucinogenic drug. A number of well-known works by Louis Wain, Nijinsky and Kurelek are included in the collection. The collection is in the custody of the Maudsley Hospital, London.

Highcroft Hospital, Birmingham

Art Therapist: Teresa Lisin

I try to create atmosphere that is comfortable, relaxing and friendly. I allow absolute freedom to use available art media. I encourage but never press patients. I also try to develop the rehabilitative aspects of patients' work in the therapy room. I hope to inspire confidence as far as possible.

Highgate Centre, London

Art Therapist: Maureen Cantwell

Clients are encouraged to interpret their own work and talk about what they have done. The painting often acts as a catalyst. When a client begins to recognise what his symbols mean, he is able to talk about what lies in his unconscious and by free association sometimes recalls long repressed memories. It may take some time to recognise what the symbols are about and some help from the knowledge of the client and his previous work, to suggest what they might be about. Just as the client's unconscious is expressed in dreams and fantasies, so spontaneous painting is a reflection of the inner self.

The spontaneous painting is a mirror image of the unconscious, thus the client is brought face to face with himself. It is sometimes valuable for him to identify with the symbols in the picture, especially when he is unaware why he has put them there. This allows him to accept responsibility for what he has done and sometimes to accept those parts of himself he would otherwise prefer not to recognise. This method of talking through a painting is particularly useful to the more withdrawn client who might find difficulty in speaking about or recognising his feelings in a 'talking' group, yet is helped to express himself quite freely when he has something tangible to talk through.

For some clients art therapy is mostly supportive; there exists a simple acceptance between the client, his work and the therapist. This acceptance allows some clients to release some of their repressed emotions, whereas for others, it means expressing the 'here and now'. There is understanding and respect for what is left unsaid. Some clients prefer not to talk about what they have done but just want acceptance for who they are.

Art therapy does away with sophistication, allows freedom, allows the child to emerge

and be accepted. It often allows the client to gain valuable insight and perhaps stirs a forgotten memory. Sometimes the recognition of what lies within can be disturbing.
It can be valuable for the client to look back on his work as a series so that he can see the change that has taken place. I feel very much that spontaneous painting is like a dream expressing and reflecting where the person is at; symbols are produced which gradually unfold to help the individual know, understand and accept himself for the person he is.

Hill End Hospital, St. Albans

Art Therapist: Myra Cohen

In the large area of our art therapy department we try to maintain a quality of quiet in which an individual with support and encouragement is able to explore the powerful field of subjective emotion through the media of paint, clay and poetry. All work whether subjective or otherwise is considered valuable as an expression of the person's state of mind at that time.

Ingrebourne Centre, St George's Hospital, Hornchurch, Essex

Art Therapist: Gerry McNeilly

The Ingrebourne Centre is a psychotherapeutic community specifically involved with the age group of late teens to early 50s mainly in the neurosis areas. I have been the sole art therapist for the past year. The work submitted is a study of how pictures the patients have made of people who influence them change after a 3-4 month period of community therapy.

Knowle Hospital, Hampshire

Art Therapist: Anna Goldsmith

In art therapy the process of making art contains many divergent possibilities and how these are utilised depends on the presence of trust within the therapeutic relationship. Once this is established the art therapist may, with the patient's confidence, be allowed to share in the process of change.
I see my function, at least, to be to provide a safe structure for the work process—positive development of an individual or group. Aims and techniques are dependent on the needs of the patient and what else is available to them in their setting.
I prefer to use art therapy with an individual as an adjunct to the work they may do in psychotherapy and I have found this to be successful but not always possible (or necessary) for all patients. Others may use the session to find space for themselves, to take stock, to be expressive, or simply to enjoy the possibility of making things.

Marlborough Hospital, London

Art Therapist: Patricia Nowell-Hall

The art of creativity is therapeutic itself. Especially for those who feel deeply unsure of their relation to themselves and to other people and are isolated from their surroundings, it can be a vital means of self-expression and communication often succeeding where words fail. Working with materials in this way can lead to greater experience and awareness of oneself in relation to something external. One can call on one's own inner world of images—making a bridge between inner and outer—and on one's own potential for inner healing and harmony. This can lead to the establishment of a greater sense of identity and value as a uinque and special individual.
At the Marlborough therapists work both with individuals and with groups. In the groups the patients can share their discovery of others thereby learning to interact with and trust others more fully.
I see my role as art therapist as being a catalyst and facilitator rather than being an

instructor or analyst. The main aim is to help people to explore themselves and get in touch with their own hidden self, to find their own expression and understanding through the images they produce. An examination of paintings made through a course of therapy can often reveal the beginnings of deep psychic change. I feel that art in therapy can be very valuable not only in itself but also as a complementary activity for psychotherapeutic treatment.

Paddington Centre for Psychotherapy

Art Therapist: Diane Waller

Diane Waller is also a lecturer in art therapy at Goldsmiths' College, London.

The art therapy department at the Paddington Centre for Psychotherapy takes patients from the adult out-patient department and the day hospital. These patients are predominantly male and have psychoneurotic problems, including agoraphobia, depression, anxiety, alcoholism, drug abuse, obsessions and sexual problems. Treatment at the centre is entirely through psychotherapy. Once admitted patients may be referred to art therapy by their psychiatrist or in the case of day hospital patients they refer themselves.

Art therapy provides patients with an opportunity to use drawing, painting, modelling and printmaking as means of self-expression and of gaining insight into, and acceptance of, their emotional state. As the work presented here indicates, some patients have discovered that they can develop their personal creativity in the secure non-judgemental atmosphere of the art department, even though the art therapists regard their work primarily as psychodynamic and do not aim to produce artists. At present there are three art therapists employed working both on a one-to-one basis and with groups.

Springfield Hospital, London

Art Therapist: Robin Holton

The art therapy department in a psychiatric hospital is often an asylum within an asylum. That is to say it is a refuge from the depersonalising manoeuvres of a large institution and its agents.

It also provides people with space to express inconvenient or unspeakable feelings. The relationship between an art therapist and the hospital that employs him is often abrasive. It can scarcely be otherwise since it often happens that people paint their best pictures when they are most 'ill' and the pictures often get worse as a person gets 'better'. This paradox is central to art therapy.

Young People's Unit, Parkside Hospital, Macclesfield

Art Therapist: Nigel Mottram

The primary aims of art therapy in the Young People's Unit are:

a. To encourage the young people to gain confidence in, and to learn to enjoy, the various materials at their disposal.
b. To enable the young people to get to the stage where they are able to make decisions as to what materials and colours (if any) they are going to use for a particular theme, and to enable them to experiment with the materials.
c. As their confidence grows, to encourage them to talk casually and freely with each other about the project they are engaged upon.
d. To develop their creative potential and, through the above aims, to express with genuine awareness and feeling their fantasies, dreams, desires, or any other particular theme that they may be interested in.
e. The ultimate general aim is, through the development of the imagination, and a keener appreciation of external things which at first sight appear mundane, to create a deeper awareness of themselves as individuals and their environment inside and outside the unit.

Any act of creativity is quite often a personal and private form of dialogue within the person involved, and which is expressed visually. Because of the very fact that the 'emotion' felt has to be stated visually, rather than in debate, it cannot always be explained adequately in words.
Paintings done in art therapy often represent attempts by people who find the world confusing and disturbed to create a stable object. This is not simple; it requires concentration and perception, faculties young people find difficult to use.

Warley Hospital, Brentwood

Art Therapist: Walter Stone

My aim in art therapy is to provide a milieu that allows individuals to become progressively aware and accepting of their intrinsic strengths, weaknesses and fears—that form part of any personality. Through creative activities, encouraged and assisted by the therapist, such fears or erroneous ideas become represented and achieve tangible form. This realisation can remove obstacles to inner growth of the personality and allow individuals to achieve a greater harmony of inner and outer realities, that is to balance the demands of the society in which they live with their own inner strivings.

West Cheshire Psychiatric Hospital

Art Therapist: Sarah Griffith

I feel art therapy aims ideally at assisting an integration or reintegration of the personality, a relationship between the Self and the World, by the use of the materials of the visual arts. Art and therapy may both be approached subjectively by a disturbed person. In art the subjective approach consists of letting the inner state of being be expressed in the medium; in therapy this approach allows the person to become the agent in his or her own healing process instead of being the passive recipient of treatment.

Illustration 9

Illustration 10

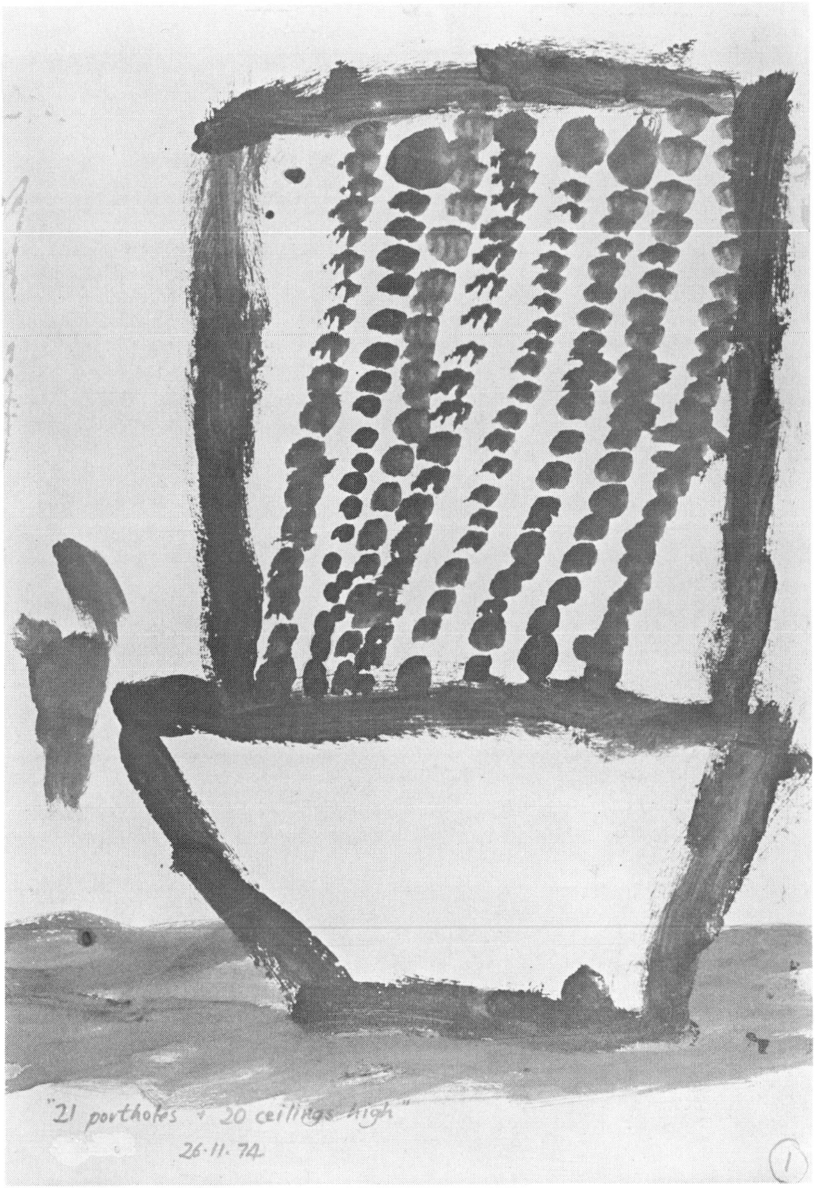

Illustration 11

Notes on the illustrations

1. *Portrait of Diaghilev.* A crayon caliper drawing made by Nijinsky during his schizophrenic illness.
   Copyright: Guttmann Maclay Collection.
2. *Model putting on a stocking.* A pastel drawing made by a long-stay patient in his early thirties. His illness is schizophrenic and shows evidence of sexual disturbance.
   Collection: Peter Byrne.
3. *Head.* Drawing by a male patient, late twenties. Schizophrenic illness. Possibly a psychotic self-portrait.
   Springfield Hospital, London.
4. *My bedroom when a little girl.* Charcoal drawing by an anorexic teenage girl.
   Glenside Hospital, Bristol.
5. Work by a depressed withdrawn lady who rarely offered any spontaneous verbal communication or interacted in any way with patients or staff. The rigid organisation of the structure of the design maintains the safe emotional isolation of individual objects and people.
   Collection: Hertfordshire College of Art and Design.
6. *Man in a helmet.* Pencil and gouache drawing made by a boy aged nine. The man's eyes are not visible behind an armour-plated visor.
   Collection: Diana Halliday.
7. *The Four Upright Citizens of the World.* Watercolour made by a Ukrainian emigré who was admitted into a large London hospital in 1934 just after the war. His work chronicles events of the time and expresses his own personal feelings and grievances against society.
   Collection: Christine Walker.
8. *Mother and Aunts.* Pencil and crayon drawing made in the 1950s when the patient was about twenty one. His works epitomise 'the creative illness' and have been exhibited in commercial galleries. He has suffered periodic depressions during one of which he buried his pictures in his garden. Stanley Leach
   Collection: Peter Byrne.

9,10 These gouache paintings of landscapes were made by an epileptic male patient in his early 30s. He categorised and documented his fits over a period of two years. He was found drowned in a pond at the age of 35.
Collection: Peter Byrne.

11. *Ship.* One of a series of obsessive gouaches on the theme of ships and swimming pools (see cover also) made by a nine year old autistic boy. In all of these works statistics and dimensions (21 portholes and 20 ceilings high) are given.
    Collection: Hertfordshire College of Art and Design.

Baines *The Mythology of the Soul*, deals with two artistic patients.

Bibliography

Allderidge, P., *The Late Richard Dadd*, London, 1974.

Anderson, W., ed. *Therapy and the Arts. Tools of Consciousness,* New York, 1977. A useful compendium of essays on many aspects of the use of therapy and the arts.

Barnes, M. and Berke, J. H., *Mary Barnes. Two Accounts of a Journey through Madness*, London, 1971.

Breton, A., *L'Art des fous, la clé des champs*, Paris, 1953.

British Association of Art Therapists, *Art and therapy*, London, n.d.

Cardinal, R., *Outsider Art*, London, 1972.

Champernowne, H. I., 'Creative Expression and Ultimate Values', introduced by Dr. A. Stevens, *American Journal of Art Therapy*, Vol. 16, October 1976.

Commonwealth Institute, *Art and mental health*, London, 1968.

Dubuffet, J., ed. *L'Art brut*, nos. 1-8, Paris, 1964-66.

Ehrenzweig, A., *The Hidden Order of Art*, London, 1967.

Evans, J., *A questionnaire survey of the role and function of Art Therapists in the National Health Service in England and Wales*, St. Albans (Hertfordshire College of Art and Design), 1977.

Freud, S., *Introductory Lectures in Psychoanalysis*, London, 1973 (first published, Vienna, 1915).

Freud, S., *Leonardo*, introduction by B. Farrell, Harmondsworth (Pelican), 1963.

Fry, R., *The Art of Psychoanalysis*, London, 1924.

Haslam, J., *Illustrations of Madness exhibiting a singular case of insanity,* London, 1810. *

Hill, A., *Art versus Illness—A study of Art Therapy*, London, 1948.

Institute of Contemporary Arts, *Art as communication*, London, 1964.

Jung, C. G., *Man and his Symbols*, London, 1964.

Jung, C. G., *Modern Man in Search of a Soul*, New York, London, 1933.

Keyes, M., *The Inward Journey—Art as Therapy for You*, California, 1974.

Kramer, E., *Art as therapy with children*, New York, 1971.

Kris, E., *Psychoanalytic Explorations in Art*, New York, 1952.

Lindsay, Z., *Art and the Handicapped Child*, London, 1972.

Lombroso, C., *Genio e follia*, Turin, 1882.

Lydiatt, E. M., *Spontaneous Painting and Modelling*, London, 1971.

Milner, M., *On Not Being Able to Paint*, London, 1950.

Naumberg, M., *Dynamically Orientated Art Therapy*, New York, 1966.

Navratil, L., *Schizophrenie und Kunst*, Munich, 1965.

Pickford, R. W., *Psychology and Visual Aesthetics*, London, 1972.

Pickford, R. W., *Studies in Psychoanalytic Art*, Illinois, 1967.

Prinzhorn, H., *Artistry of the Mentally Ill,* English language edition, New York, 1972 (first published 1922).

* reproduced, said Peter Byrne, in McAlpine & Hunter's book — the first single-case study.

Prinzhorn, H., *Art Therapy*, New York, 1975.
Rainer, A., 'Katatonenkunst', *Manuskripte*, Graz, 1969.
Rainer, A., 'Euthanasie der Kunst', *Neues Forum*, Vienna, 1969.
Rainer, A., 'Die 13. Muse oder Wahnsinn eine Kunstart', *Jahrbuch Protokolle*, Vienna, 1970.
Rave-Schwank, M., Broekman, J., Rothe, W., *Bildnerei der Geisteskranken aus der Prinzhorn-Sammlung*, Heidelberg, 1967.
Réja, M., *L'Art chez les fous*, Paris, 1905.
Spector, J., *The Aesthetics of Freud*, New York, 1970.
Stokes, A., *Selected writings—The image in form*, an anthology edited by Richard Wollheim.
Ulman, E., and Dachinger, P., ed. *Art Therapy in Theory and Practice*, New York, 1975.
Volmat, R., *L'Art psychopathologique*, Paris, 1956. Contains an important bibliography.
Winnicott, D. W., *Playing and Reality*, London, 1971.

Contributors to the catalogue

Peter Byrne trained as an artist and is involved in postgraduate research into art therapy at Birmingham Polytechnic.

Michael Edwards trained as an art therapist with Irene Champernowne at the Withymead Centre and is Senior Lecturer in Art Therapy at Birmingham Polytechnic.

Diana Halliday has worked for a number of years as an art therapist in child guidance clinics and is a lecturer in art therapy at Hertfordshire College of Art and Design.

John Henzell has worked as an art therapist in psychiatric hospitals, and is researching into the history of psychopathology and art.